Python Programming for Beginners
- Book 1

The Crash Course You Need to Learn the Basics of Python and How to Work With Files, Classes & Objects, Even if You Have Never Written a Line of Code Before.

Martin Evans

Committee of Publishers Association and is legally binding throughout the United States.

Furthermore, the transmission, duplication, or reproduction of any of the following work including specific information will be considered an illegal act irrespective of if it is done electronically or in print. This extends to creating a secondary or tertiary copy of the work or a recorded copy and is only allowed with an expressed written consent from the Publisher. All additional right reserved.

The information in the following pages is broadly considered to be a truthful and accurate account of facts and as such any inattention, use, or misuse of the information in question by the reader will render any resulting actions solely under their purview. There are no scenarios in which the publisher or the original author of this work can be in any fashion deemed liable for any hardship or damages that may befall them after undertaking information described herein.

Additionally, the information in the following pages is intended only for informational purposes and should thus be thought of as universal. As befitting its nature, it is presented without assurance regarding its prolonged validity or interim quality. Trademarks that are mentioned are done without written consent and can in no way be considered an endorsement from the trademark holder.

Table of Contents

Python Programming 1

for Beginners...1

- Book 1..1

Table of Contents.....................................7

Introduction.. 9

Chapter 1: Getting Started with Python 12

Chapter 2: What are Some of the Basics of

Python Codes? 27

Chapter 3: Creating Your First Program.. 39

Chapter 4: How to Work with Files on

Python 43

Chapter 5: Working with Classes and

Objects.. 60

Chapter 6: How to Work with Exception

Handling 77

Chapter 7: Using Operators in Your Code 97

Conclusion 109

Introduction

Congratulations on downloading this book and thank you for doing so.

The following chapters will discuss everything that you need to know when you are getting started with the Python language. There are a lot of different coding languages that you are able to choose from, and all of them will have different features, different powers, and more. But when it comes to choosing a coding language that has all the features and power that you are looking for while also being easy for a beginner to work with, this is the coding language that is the best for you.

This guidebook will provide you with all the information that you need in order to get started with the Python language. Inside, you will learn what Python is all about, how it works, how to work with making your first code, the importance of working with classes and objects, and even how to work with exception handling. All of these will come together to provide you with some of the basics that you need to start learning how to work with the Python language.

When you are ready to start learning a new coding language and you want to pick one that has a large community, is easy to read, and is good for a beginner even though it still has a lot of power, then make sure to check out this guidebook and learn everything that you need to know to get started in Python.

There are plenty of books on this subject on the market, thanks again for choosing this one! Every effort was made to ensure it is full of as much useful information as possible. Please enjoy!

Chapter 1: Getting Started with Python

Learning a new coding language can be a great experience. It will allow you to understand how your system works better than before. It will help you to make some of your own programs without having to rely on someone else to help you out. And it can even help you to troubleshoot some of the issues that may be occurring on your own computer.

If this is the first time that you are learning a new programming language, then Python is one of the best choices to go with. It is easy to learn and use no matter which platform you are dealing with. It even has a lot of variety when it comes to the codes that you are able to work on with this coding language. And you are able to work with the Python network because it is free, which makes it simple to use while creating your own programs, finding solutions to problems in your system, or even taking care of a computer program.

In addition, even as a beginner, you will be able to read and write in this coding language. It is so easy to use, and you will be able to use it on whichever operating system that you already have on your computer. You do not need to spend time adding a new operating system to your computer in the hopes of getting the coding all done because this works the best with all of them. Now, if you are looking for a new computer and trying to pick out a good operating system, then it is a good idea to pick a Linux system, but it will work out well with any of them.

When Python was first developed a few decades ago, a team of volunteers was charged with running this program. This is considered an open source program, so this makes it easy for anyone to take the program and do what they would like with it. Any programmer will be able to make adjustments or other changes as is needed. This is why you will be able to find a few different versions of the Python language. As issues start to come up with one version, or a programmer comes up with a new development, they are able to make changes and bring out something new for you to use.

While this is the perfect language for beginners to work with, there are a lot of uses that you can enjoy with this language. You can go look online, and it won't take long before you find some websites that rely on the Python to help them to run. Sites like YouTube and Google, as well as a few other ones, were used with a bit of Python code. There are many others that use this code because it is so simple to use but has all the power that is needed.

There are a lot of benefits that you will be able to enjoy when it comes to using the Python language rather than a different coding language. Beginners like to work with Python because it is easy to learn and they will be able to pick up on it quickly, even if they are new to programming.

The Python code is considered open sourced and free. This means that you are able to start coding without having to pay any money. There are some IDLE's that you can choose that cost a little bit of money, but you can also pick out versions that are free that can help you out as well.

In addition, if you are a beginner and you need some help learning how to work with Python and how to get it to work the way that you would like, or you are stuck on a code and need some help, you will love that there are lots of communities for this language full of people who are willing to give you a hand. Python is actually really popular, which means that you will be able to find a lot of people who can answer your questions as well as some tutorials that can make coding easier.

If you need it at some point, the Python code is able to combine with some other coding languages to become stronger and more versatile. Python is strong, but there are some things that it is not that powerful. But when you are able to combine Python with another language, such as C++ and JavaScript, you will be able to get so much more done out of your codes.

While there are many things that you will love about Python, it is important to understand that it is a beginner language, so some of the more complex things that you would like to do with this language may not be possible. But as a beginner, you probably won't be able to get to these options right at the start anyway, and you can at least use Python as a stepping stone to learning one of the other languages. There are still many other things that you are able to do with Python, so you should be able to create some of the programs that you want.

Overall, for a beginner, Python is one of the best coding languages to work with. It has a simple code and syntax that you will catch on to quickly, and it isn't hard to put this to work for you.

The Top Reasons to use Python

There are a lot of different reasons that you are able to choose to go with Python. This is one of the best options on the market and will help you to get a lot of things done from troubleshooting on your own computer to writing your own codes and programs to so much more. Some of the benefits of using Python include the following:

- *Easy to work with*: Out of all the coding languages, this is one of the easiest languages for you to enjoy. You will have a good network to help you out, and the coding itself is easy to catch on to.

- *Codes in English language*: Unlike some of the other languages, you will be able to read the Python language because it is written in English. Some of the other languages will use codes and symbols that are hard to understand and can make learning a new language even more difficult than before.

- *Work with other coding languages*: While there is a lot of power that comes with working in Python, there will be some times when you are not able to get the results that you want just by working with this coding language. The good news is that you will be able to combine it with some other coding languages, such as JavaScript, in order to get that extra power and functionality to get things done.

- *Lots of power*: There is actually a lot of power that comes with using the

Python language. While this is sometimes considered just a beginners' language, there is some power that comes behind it. In fact, you will be able to find that a lot of your favorite programs and websites already used Python to help them to run.

- *Big library to work with*: The Python library will become your best friend when you are coding in this language. You will be able to look through this library at any time and get the answers that are needed to some of your questions or to learn how to get things done. Most beginners will spend a lot of time going through this library to help them get started.

- *Big community to help you out*: There are times when you are first starting when you will have questions or need help learning how to do some new coding along the way. There are a lot of people who will work with the Python language, and this makes it the perfect option to get the help that you need. Any time that you get stuck or you have a question that you need help with, then you can go online and find the right Python community to help you to be successful.

- *Object-Oriented Programming*: This may sound like a complicated thing to deal with, but it is actually pretty simple and can make your coding much easier. It allows you a simple way to organize your code so that it makes more sense and will ensure that your programming will work the way that you want. We will talk about how the classes and objects in this type of programming work so that you can see how easy it is to get everything to work together.

As you can see, there are a lot of different reasons why you will fall in love with the Python language. While this is a relatively newer language and it can sometimes be considered a simple beginners' language to work with, there is a lot of power that comes with using Python, and you will be able to do a lot of fun things with this coding language. Whether you are looking to get started in coding for the first time or you are interested in adding a new coding language to your portfolio, Python is the answer that you are sure to enjoy.

Getting Python set up

Now that you know a little bit more about Python, it is time to learn how you are able to get this program set up and downloaded on your computer so that you can start using it. There are a few steps that you have to take, and the first is that you need to pick out the version that you are allowed to work on. To see these versions, you simply need to go and visit www.python.org/downloads. From here, you are able to pick out the version that you would like to work with, and then

Python will download for you as you follow the prompts.

In addition to downloading from the Python website, it is also important that you pick out and set up the IDE (Integrated Development Environment) that you will use with Python. This IDE is the environment that you will work on in order to write your codes and do your work inside. If you do not have this, it will be impossible to get the program to work. There are some great IDRs to work with but check to see if there is a text editor that you can work with. For those who are in Windows computers, you can use Notepad, or you can find another text editor of your choice.

There are a variety of options that you can choose when it comes to the IDE and the text writer that you want to work with. It is possible to find some that are free or you can choose to go with some that you have to pay a little bit for, but then they will offer some more great features.

Once all of these things are downloaded, it is time to learn how to write some of your own codes. Python is an easy language to learn how to use, and this guidebook will share some of the basics that you should know to help you get started.

Chapter 2: What are Some of the Basics of Python Codes?

Working with the Python code is a great way to learn something new and to gain access to creating your own programs. Python has a lot of power behind it, and you will be able to pick out how complicated that you would like the code to be. Some of them will only include a few lines, and you will be able to learn those pretty quickly. Others will take up a few lines and may take some more technical knowledge, but these are still pretty simple to learn as well.

No matter what kind of code that you are trying to design with Python, there will be some common elements that are found in each of them. This chapter will take some time to look at the various parts that come with a Python code to help you to get started.

Python Keywords

The first thing that we will look at is the keywords that you can use in Python. These keywords are meant to tell the compiler how you would like it to behave. If you place them in the wrong part of the code, or you use them in the improper way, it will make some errors in your code.

These keywords are meant to be the command centers that the compiler will follow. They need to be reserved because they mean something important to the compiler, and when you do not use them in the proper way, then you are just going to mess things up and make the compiler upset. Learning the keywords and using them in the proper way will ensure that you get the codes to work the way that you want.

Naming Identifiers

When you are working with Python programming, you will find that there are a few different identifiers that you are able to work with. You may find that they go by different names and work inside the code in different ways, but they all have important roles when it comes to making the code work the way that it should. Some of the names that you will see pertaining to these identifiers include functions, classes, entities, and variables.

When you are working on naming one of these identifiers, you will be able to stick with the same name and rules no matter which one you are working with. This helps to make it easier to remember the rules.

When it comes to naming these identifiers, you have to watch out for the way that you do it. There are quite a few names that you can pick for these, and you are able to use uppercase and lowercase letters along with numbers and the underscore. As long as you stick with a combination of these, then you will be fine. However, you must make sure that you are never starting the identifier name with a number, and there should not be any spaces that come in between the words if you choose more than one. Also, none of the keywords should be in the name, or you will get an error in the code.

Outside of these following easy rules, you will find that there are still a ton of names that you can choose to work with, so naming these identifiers is not going to be difficult. If you do forget one of the rules and then try to name the identifier, then you will get a syntax error on your compiler and will have to go back through and restart.

Control Flow in Python Coding

Another thing that you need to consider when you are working in the Python code is how the flow of control will work so that the compiler is able to read what you are trying to do. There are several strings of code that you must write out in a specific way to ensure that the compiler is able to execute what you want it done. You will want to write out your code like a list of instructions so that the compiler is able to keep up. Think of your code writing like working on a recipe or an instruction manual. You will need to first write down what you would like it done, then the second thing, and then the third until you are all done.

Statements

Statements are basically the strings of code that you are writing out. When you tell the compiler to do something inside of the code, you will find that those are considered statements. As long as you are able to write them out the proper way, the compiler can read them and will show the message on the computer screen. You can keep the statements pretty simple with just a few words or they could include the full block of code. You will see quite a few of these statements as you work through the examples that we provide in this guidebook.

Comments

Comments are a neat little thing that you are able to add into your code in order to explain it out a little bit to the other person who may want to look over the code. These are not going to show up in the actual code when it is executed, but it can be nice to have to ensure that the other programmers understand what each point of code is all about.

You can think of these comments like little notes that you want to leave behind inside of your code. Any other programmer who takes a look at your code will be able to read through these comments and use these notes to help them understand what you were trying to do. In order to work with a comment, you simply need to provide the (#) symbol right in front of the comment.

When this is seen by the compiler, it will decide to just skip over it and not read anything.

You are allowed to add in as many of these comments as you would like without messing up the program at all. As long as the # sign is in front of the comment, you can keep adding them in to help explain what you are doing inside your code. It is often best to keep the comments down a little bit and only use the ones that are the most important because this will make the code cleaner and easier to read, but you can add in as many as you would like.

Variables

The next thing that you are able to work with is known as variables. These will be put to use in the majority of your codes, so it is a good idea to learn how to use them properly. These variables will be in charge of helping you to store some of your values which will, in turn, make sure that the code is able to stay as nice and organized as possible. You will easily be able to add in some values to the variable with the help of the equal (=) sign, and you can sometimes even add in two or more values to the same variable depending on what you want to get done.

Operators

Operators are pretty simple parts of your code, but you should still know how they work. You will find that there are actually a few different types of them that work well. For example, the arithmetic functions are great for helping you to add, divide, subtract, and multiply different parts of the code together. There are assignment operators that will assign a specific value to your variable so that the compiler knows how to treat this. There are also comparison operators that will allow you to look at a few different pieces of code and then determine if they are similar or not and how the computer should react based on that information.

These are just a few of the different parts that you will see when you work on your Python code. These are all going to add in some of the power that you are looking for in this network and can ensure that you are getting the code to work the way that you want. Make sure to check out some more about this guidebook, and when you see some of the codes that are available in this guidebook, you will quickly be able to check and see whether these are present inside these codes or not.

Chapter 3: Creating Your First Program

It is important to take some time to learn how to code a bit in Python. It is scary sometimes when you first get started because you may think that writing out the codes will be too hard. This chapter will take the time to look at a basic code to use that will make it easier for you to learn how to work with Python. Here, we will look at the Hello World code.

Let us assume that you have already visited the Python website and downloaded the version that you want to use for this programming language. It is often best to go with the newest version because this will save you a lot of time and hassle and will make sure that you are getting the newest and best features.

The first thing that you should take a look at in order to write out your first code is to open up an IDE. You will be able to go into the Python-installed directory in the command prompt. Then, you need to understand which program you picked out. This will matter because the syntax that you use to write out the codes will depend on which version of your interpreter under Python that you went with.

Now, make sure that you have your text editor open; it is time to write out the code. You will just write out the word print first because this is the keyword that will tell the

40

compiler that you want it to list the statement that you put out following it. Whatever you place after the print word will be is what will show up on your screen. So, in this example, you will want to write out the following code in your compiler:

print ("Hello, world!")

When you have written this out, you will then need to hit Enter. Then when you decide that you are ready to run your program, you will see the phrase "Hello, world!" show up on the screen.

Now, you are able to go through and change this around as much as you would like. If you have some other sentences that you would like to have come up on the screen, then the sentence can be long or short as long as you use the example above as your template to make it easier.

As you can see, writing out some of your own codes can be easy when you are working with Python. The example above helped you to print a message on the screen, and it only took a few minutes. Of course, there will be much more complicated codes that you can work on in this language, but this at least gives you a good idea of how to get started. Go ahead and open up your compiler and give this one a try to see how it works for you.

Chapter 4: How to Work with Files on Python

Now that we have taken some time to look at the basic parts that come with Python, it is time to work with some of your files using this programming language. When you first start to learn how to work with a new code, you will be creating something new, and you will want to ensure that Python is able to sore that data in a way that you can easily access it whenever you need it. When you get it saved inside of Python, you will want to make sure that the information will show up inside of your code at the proper time. This chapter will help you learn how to do all of these in the proper way so that the code works properly.

Whenever you are ready to store some data for your code, you are basically going to create a file, even though there will be some times when it is a good idea to reuse that block of code again in the same code. There are different operations that you are able to choose from in order to make this all work. In this chapter, we will work on what is called file mode. To do all of these, think about when you are working on Word and how you will be able to create new files, save them, modify them, and more. This is the same idea of what we will do in this chapter. Some of the different things that you are able to do with your files when you are coding in Python include the following:

- Close a file

- Edit a file so that it has some more code
- Move a file
- Create a new file

Let's take a look at how you can do these different tasks to help you get started with your files in Python.

Creating a File

The first task that we will take a look at is how you would create a new file to use. If you want to write on the new file before you save it, you should make sure that you have opened the file, and then you have to check that you are on writing mode to help you out. You should notice that Python has three different choices for you when it comes to writing inside of your opened file including mode(x), write(w), and append(a). If you want to get started with writing your code in the file, you would rely on the write(w) mode to get it all done.

If you open up a new file and you are ready to write out some statements or a few strings to go inside of it, like when you are ready to write your code or some binary files, then you will just need to open up the write(w) mode as well. This write(w) method is the best option because you are able to bring it out and just start writing the code like you are writing in a Word document which makes it easier for a lot of people to get started.

Out of the three options that you are using, the write(w) one will be one of the easiest that you can use. It is easy to start up a new file by writing things out on the code, or you can even use this in order to make some changes that are inside your files that are already full. But for now, we will focus on how you can use this write(w) function in order to get a brand new file started in your code:

#file handling operations
#writing to a new file hello.txt
f = open('hello.txt', 'w', encoding = 'utf-8')
f.write("Hello Python Developers!")
f.write("Welcome to Python World")
f.flush()
f.close()

Take the time to write out the code above in the text editor and let it execute. With this code, you will tell your compiler that you want the information that is placed into your new file to go into the current directory. You are doing this because the code does not originally specify where the content should go, so you will use this part to make sure that you are able to find where the information is later on.

After you have typed in this code, you should be able to go through your current directory and see if you are able to find the information there. You can then open up the file. If everything was typed in the right way, then you will get the message "Hello Python Developers! Welcome to Python World!" on the screen.

Now that you have had a chance to write out this easy code, we will take it a little further in the next step. Let's say that you are working on your code and you decide that it is time to change up some of the information that you already placed into the code. With the example that we did above, we will simply change something about the message that shows up on the screen. As long as you stick with the write(w) function again, you will not have too many troubles getting it to work. Take a look at the following code to see how this should be done.

```
#file handling operations
#writing to a new file hello.txt
f = open('hello.txt', 'w', encoding = 'utf-8')
f.write("Hello Python Developers!")
f.write("Welcome to Python World")
```

mylist = ["Apple", "Orange", "Banana"]
#writelines() is used to write multiple lines
into the file
f.write(mylist)
f.flush()
f.close()

Now, we are keeping things pretty simple when we write out this code, but it is a good way to show that there are some different changes inside of the file. For this example, we are just adding in one more line, and you are able to keep going with this idea to place in as many lines as you would like. Take a moment to put this information into your compiler and see what comes up. If you did this the right way, you should get a new message on your screen that says "Hello

Python Developers! Welcome to Python World. Apple Orange Banana."

Working with Binary Files

Now, it is time to move on to another thing that you can do with your Python code which includes writing a binary file. This may sound like something a bit scary to work on, especially if you do not know much about binary files, but it is actually really easy to work with and will allow you to write out your data as a sound or image file, rather than working with text files.

You are able to take any of the text or information that you are working on in Python and write it into a binary file, no matter what kind of information was in it to start with. All files will follow the same rules and formatting to make this happen. Remember that to make your binary file, you will need to supply the data into the object form so that the compiler will take it and expose that information as a byte. Let's take a look at an example of how to get this to work below:

 # write binary data to a file
 # writing the file hello.dat write binary mode
F = open('hello.dat', 'wb')
 # writing as byte strings
f.write(b"I am writing data in binary file!/n")
f.write(b"Let's write another list/n")
f.close()

Take some time to write this code into your compiler. You will then need to open up Notepad so that you are able to see what is already written into this program. Remember that you will need to decode and also encode the functions so that they are easier to read and write once you get into the mode for binary files. To make sure that this happens, use the following syntax:

 # write binary data to a file
 # writing the file hello.dat write binary mode
f = open('hello.dat', 'wb')
text = "Hello World"
f.write(text.encode('utf-8'))
f.close()

Opening Files up in Python

After you have taken some time to design a new file and then get that file to save properly, it is time to learn how to open some of these files. It won't be that helpful for you to create a bunch of files and then save them if you are not able to open them up and use them at some point. The syntax that you need to use in order to open up the files inside of your program includes the following:

 # read binary data to a file
#writing the file hello.dat write append binary mode
with open("hello.dat", 'rb') as f:
    data = f.read()
    text = data.decode('utf-8'(

print(text)

The output that you would get from putting this into the system would be like the following:

Hello, world!
This is a demo using with
This file contains three lines
Hello world
This is a demo using with
This file contains three lines.

This example will show you what happens when you open up a specific file on your program, but that is to make sure that you get the right information to show up and to make sure that you are doing it the right way. You will be able to follow this same syntax in order to open up any file that is stored on the system. This is a simple syntax, and it is one that you should keep with you so that you are able to open up a file and read what is inside, which is a good way to start working on your own coding.

Moving Your Files

At this point, you have gotten a chance to work with files in Python. You know how to open the files, how to save the files, and even how to turn the files into binary files. Now, it is time to learn about how to move a file to a new location if your code needs it. As a beginner, you may forget that your file will be saved in the current directory if you do not specify a location in your code. But maybe you wanted to make sure that you saved that file to another directory. The good news is that it is really easy to move this file at any time so that it ends up in the location that you would like.

The trick to starting with this process is the ability to figure out where you saved the original file. If you are not sure what the current directory was when you saved that file, it can be hard to find it later on. Always look in the current directory if you are able to remember, or you may have to search around a bit to find the information that you need.

Once you have been able to locate the file that you wish to move, then open it up with the code that we talked about in the last section. While you are here, you can use the write(w) mode to help you to add in more information to the code if you need to. You can then go to the right spot and tell the code where you want to move it, and you are able to do this by giving it a new name or physically choosing where you would like the code to be placed.

There are quite a few things that you are able to do with the files in Python, and learning more about them gives you some great experience working with Python. The file system may seem pretty simple, and you may feel that you don't need to have any code to get this to happen; but codes are required to do anything in Python, and getting some practice while messing around with the files is a good way to become familiar with the syntax and code writing for some of the more complicated stuff we can do later.

With the file, you are able to write in a new file for the first time, open up a file, make some changes to the file, and even change the location of your file so that it is easier to find. All of these are simple steps that a beginner can handle and you will be able to get some familiarity with the compiler and some of the other things that come with writing your code inside of Python!

Chapter 5: Working with Classes and Objects

Python is one of the languages that is considered an Object Oriented Programming language (OOP). Basically, this means that this language is designed to be easier for a beginner to handle. The classes and objects inside of the language will work together so that you are able to keep things in line and as organized as possible in your code.

To make things simple, the classes can be thought of as containers that will place all the objects together. You are able to pick which objects will go together in each class, but it is important that the objects that are in the same class will have something in common and make sense that they are in the same class. These objects are all going to be pulled up at the same time inside of your code, so it helps to organize them this way.

When you are working with Python, you will be able to make the objects that go into each class whatever you would like. With that said, it is a good idea to place objects that are similar in the same class because this will help you organize them and can make the code work more efficiently. This doesn't mean that you have to have the objects be exactly the same. However, when someone takes a look at your classes, they should be able to easily figure out how all the objects are related.

Now, there are a lot of things that you will be able to do with these objects and classes, but you should understand a few things before you start creating your classes including:

- Objects that you place into the same class will need to be similar in some way and not too complicated to figure out how they are related. They don't have to be identical though. For example, you could have a class that holds onto fruits and then place things like pears, apples, peaches, bananas, and grapes inside.

- Classes are good to learn about because they are the blueprint and the design for the objects because they are the parts that will be in charge of telling the interpreter how you want it to run the program.

How to Create a Class

Now that we have taken a bit to learn the basics of classes and objects, it is time to learn how to create these classes. This is a pretty simple process to work with once you have the right syntax to help you. To start, you need to make sure that you are creating a new definition for each class at the same time. When you are working on a class, it is important to place the name that you are giving to your class right after the keyword, and then you will be able to place the superclass inside of your parenthesis. Then you can add in a colon so that you can keep up with what is considered good coding practices. Below is a good example of how you can use the right syntax to help you create your new Python class:

```
class Vehicle(object):
#constructor
def_init_(self, steering, wheels, clutch, breaks, gears):
self._steering = steering
self._wheels = wheels
self._clutch = clutch
self._breaks =breaks
self._gears  = gears
#destructor
def_del_(self):
    print("This is destructor....")


#member functions or methods
```

```
def Display_Vehicle(self):
    print('Steering:' , self._steering)
    print('Wheels:', self._wheels)
    print('Clutch:', self._clutch)
    print('Breaks:', self._breaks)
    print('Gears:', self._gears)
#instantiate a vehicle option
myGenericVehicle    =    Vehicle('Power
Steering', 4, 'Super Clutch', 'Disk Breaks', 5)
myGenericVehicle.Display_Vehicle()
```

The output that you will be able to get from putting all of this information into your interpreter includes the following:

('Steering:', 'Power Steering')
('Wheels:', 4)
('Clutch:'. 'Super Clutch')
('Breaks:', 'Disk Breaks')

('Gears:', 5)

Take some time to type in this example into your compiler and see what happens. There are a lot of parts that are present. First, you will be able to see the definition of the object, and then the attributes and the method definition. This is followed by the class definition, the destructor function, and then the function. Now, this will sound a little bit confusing, so we will start out by seeing how each of these parts work and how they are able to help you to create classes.

Class Definition and Object Instantiation

These are both going to be important to the syntax of creating classes because they will basically tell the code what needs to happen for it to do what you want. The class definition will include the part in the syntax that says "class subclass(superclass0)" and then the part for the object instantiation will include the part that says "object = class()."

Special Attributes

Now, we need to take a look at the special attributes that come with the code. There are a few of these attributes that you can add to your code when you are working on Python.

Being able to learn about some of these attributes can help you to better create the code that you want and will ensure that the interpreter knows what you want to do in the program. Some of the most important codes that you can choose from when working in Python include the following:

__dict____   this is the direct variable of a class namespace

__doc___   this is the document reference string of class

__name____ this will be the class name

__module__   this is the module name and consists of the class

__bases__ this is the tuple that will also contain all of the superclasses

Memorizing these can help you out, but it may be nice to learn how they work inside of the code. Here is an example below that you can try out by typing into your compiler.

```
class Cat(object):
        itsWeight = 0
        itsAge = 0
        itsName = ""
        defMeow(self):
        print("Meow!")

        defDisplayCat(self):
        print("I am a Cat Object, My name is", self.itsName)
        print("My age is", self.itsAge)
        print("My weight is", self.itsWeight)

frisky = Cat()
```

frisky.itsAge = 10
frisky.itsName = "Frisky"
frisky.DisplayCat()
frisky.Meow()

When you are using this as your syntax in the interpreter, the result that you will get on the screen is the following:

('I am a Cat Object, My name is', 'Frisky')
('My age is', 10)
('My weight is', 0)
Meow!

Accessing the Members of Your Class

Looking at the examples that we worked on above, we did spend some time and identified our object, which was the cat, as being called Frisky by using the dot operator. This helped the program to access the right members of the objects. What this means is if we wanted to make sure that we were able to get the age of the cat Frisky, then we would just have to use the simple function "frisky.itsAge=1-" to make this happen. This is something that is easily done no matter which object that you are trying to assign.

If you go back and look at the code that we did above, you may notice that there were a lot of variables that were present inside of it. Sometimes, all of these variables will be inconvenient to use, and they can make the code look a little messy if you are working with a lot of them in the same code. The good news is that you are able to choose from a few different methods to use to avoid this issue. The method that most programmers will use because it is simple and easy will be the accessor information. This option will be able to provide you with the information that you need without using as much work.

It is really easy to use the accessor method to make sure that you are taking care of your variables. The syntax that you would use to make this happen includes the following:

class Cat(object)
    itsAge = None
    itsWeight = None
    itsName = None

```python
#set accessor function use to assign
values to the fields or member vars
    def setItsAge(self, itsAge):
    self.itsAge = itsAge

    def setItsWeight(self, itsWeight):
    self.itsWeight = itsWeight

    def setItsName(self, itsName):
    self.itsName =itsName

#get accessor function use to return
the values from a field
    def getItsAge(self):
    return self.itsAge
    def getItsWeight(self):
    return self.itsWeight

    def getItsName(self):
```

```
        return self.itsName

objFrisky = Cat()
objFrisky.setItsAge(5)
objFrisky.setItsWeight(10)
objFrisky.setItsName("Frisky")
print("Cats          Name          is:",
objFrisky.getItsname())
print("Its age is:", objFrisky.getItsAge())
print("Its          weight          is:",
objFrisky.getItsName())
```

The output that you will get from all of these will be the following:

```
('Cats Name is:', 'Frisky')
(Its age is:', 5)
('Its weight is:', 10)
```

In the method above, we are placing in the accessor method and then making sure that it works right with the variables that you want to use. This will work out well for when you want to work on data encapsulation or data hiding. When you want to create some accessibility to your members, make sure that some of these will be public and they are easy to access using this method, but some will be protected or private.

Working with objects and classes is a basic part of the Python code, and it can help to get a lot of great power in your codes. These classes and objects do not need to be complicated, but they are so important to help you organize your information to make it show up when the program is trying to run. Take the time to put some of the codes that we have above into your compiler and get some practice working with these.

Chapter 6: How to Work with Exception Handling

So far in this guidebook, we have spent a lot of time talking about the basics that you are able to do when you work in the Python language. You have learned what Python is all about, how to get started with this language, and even some basic codes to work on such as the Hello World code and working with objects and classes. You have a good start on working in this language and being able to get some things done inside your code.

Now that you have gotten a chance to learn about those other important aspects of working in Python, it is time to work on something that is a little more complex. In this chapter, we will learn how to handle exceptions in your code. When you are working with these exceptions, you will determine how an interpreter will react when there is a condition that the compiler sees as abnormal inside of the code. When you work with these exceptions, you will change up the conditions of the code so that you can help the computer act the way that you would like, rather than having an error come up.

Any time that you are looking to show that a condition is abnormal inside the code, it is a good idea to make sure that exceptions occur in Python There are some conditions that will be predetermined by the system, and it will not allow you to let them happen. While you are not going to be able to convince the program that these are not exceptions, you can have some say in how they are presented by the compiler. For example, if you put a statement into the code, or you misspell one of your variables, you may see that the compiler will see this as abnormal because it is not able to find what you are looking for. In addition, when you try to get your code to divide by the number zero, you would end up with an exception as well.

Normally, these exceptions will pop up and just say that there is an error in the code. This is not very informative. As you will see as we go through this chapter, there are some things that you can change in your coding to ensure that you get a message that explains what is going on, instead of leaving yourself or your user confused.

Depending on the type of code that you are trying to work on, there are times when you will want to convince the compiler to raise an exception. In this case, the situation would not necessarily be considered an exception, but you need it to be this way to work in the code that you are writing. For example, if you are working on the code for a program where you only want to allow those who are over 18 to use, you would be able to raise an exception so that when someone is younger than 18 and they try to put their information in, the website will refuse to let them in.

When you decide to work on Python as well as any of its other programs, you should stop to look at the library that comes with it. You will be able to find some of the common exceptions already listed inside. This can make it easier for the beginner to write their codes because all the information is right there.

Even when you run into an issue, you will be able to control what is going on in the code and how it behaves. If you simply leave the code alone and then an exception from the library shows up, then the compiler will show up a messy message about how an exception has happened. The biggest issue with this exception message is that it will not explain how the exception happened or what is going on. This can make things confusing for the user.

Instead of doing this, you will be able to use the idea of exception handling to tell the computer system where it is supposed to better handle those exceptions when it comes up. So, let's say that the user was going through your program, and they tried to divide by zero. Instead of having a big message coming up that is not that helpful, you could use the code to change it around so that a message like "You are trying to divide by zero!" will show up.

If you find that you want to add in an exception of your own and it is not being covered by the Python library, then it is possible for you to go through and define some of your own. When you are done doing this, the code will be able to trigger some of these new exceptions so that the program works the way that you would like. This is a great way to make sure that you are having all the control that you want while working on the code.

When it is time to bring out these neat exceptions in your code, you will need to take some time to learn how to read the terms and the keywords that come with it. These terms are so important because they will signal to the Python library that you are raising the exception in the first place. Some of the terms that you need to learn to make things easier include the following:

- Finally—this is the action that you will want to use to perform cleanup actions, whether the exceptions occur or not.
- Assert—this condition will trigger the exception inside of the code
- Raise—the raise command will trigger an exception manually inside of the code.
- Try/except—this is when you want to try out a block of code and then it is recovered thanks to the exceptions that either you or the Python code raised.

These are some of the basics that you should learn in order to use the Python exceptions in the proper way. There is so much that you can do with this information, and we will take some time to look at them and help you to learn the syntax and more that will help you to get started.

Raising Exceptions

The first thing that we need to learn how to do in this chapter is to raise these exceptions. Any time that something comes up with one of the codes that you are writing, or you discover that the program you are working on is not doing something that it is supposed to, then the Python code will raise up what is known as an exception to these activities. The reason that this happens is that the Python program is not sure how it is supposed to handle the situation on hand. Sometimes the issue is simple, and it is just that you named something wrong when you were trying to pull it up, so the code was not able to find it. Let's take a look at what will happen when you are dealing with this issue:

```
x = 10
y = 10
result = x/y #trying to divide by zero
print(result)
```

The output that you will get when you try to get the interpreter to go through this code would be the following:

```
>>>
Traceback (most recent call last):
    File "D: \Python34\tt.py", line 3, in <module>
    result = x/y
```

ZeroDivisionError: division by zero

>>>

Let's take some time to break down this example and look at how it works. In this example, the Python code will bring up an error on your screen because you are basically dividing a number by zero. This is something that the Python language is not allowed to do, so it will result in an error. Now, this will end up causing a big mess because the way that this is set up right now will provide a message on the screen that your user will not be able to comprehend. The good news is all this is that you are able to change up the code a little bit so that when the user error comes up, it will explain what is going on and won't confuse them so much.

The best thing for you to do is to add on a friendly message, so when an error occurs, the user is not going to become so confused in the process. The message can work to tell the user what mistakes they have made, and then they will know what they are supposed to do. Most of the errors that bring up exceptions will be easy to work with, such as when the user accidentally types in 0 instead of 10, so having these friendlier messages will be simple and help the user to fix the issue.

Adding in these messages can be so simple once you learn how to get them all done. The following is the syntax and an example of how you will be able to raise an exception and show a friendlier message to your user all at the same time:

```
x = 10
y = 0
result = 0
try:
    result = x/y
    print(result)
except ZeroDivisionError:
    print("You are trying to divide by
zero.")
```

Looking at the example above, you will see that we are still working with the exception that we did above. You are still going to have an error showing up in your code, but instead of sending over a message that is confusing and doesn't tell your user anything about what happened, you will send over a simple message that tells them what is going on. You can add anything that you would like to the message, but it is often best if you stick with something that is short and sweet to make it easier.

Defining Your Personal Exceptions

With the work that we did above, we were working with an exception that is already recognized inside of the Python library. The program is automatically not going to let this happen and it will send out the first message if you do not change things up like we showed. You don't have to go through any work to tell the system that there should be an exception in there.

Depending on the type of code that you are working on and what you would like it to do, there may be times when you need to create your own exceptions. These will be unique because, under normal circumstances, Python would allow these to happen without any errors. But to make sure that the code works the way that you want, you will want to tell Python to make these circumstances exceptions.

For example, when you are working on a code, you may want to design it so that the user is not allowed to put in specific numbers. You would easily be able to add an exception to the code to make this happen. Or if you want to allow the user to guess an answer to a question five times before the program moves on, you would be able to do this as well. The input that the user is trying to use doesn't have to be wrong to the

Python, but because of the way that you set up your code, you will want to add in the exceptions so that the program responds to how you want.

There are not that many limits on what kinds of exceptions that you are able to add into the code, but they do need to make sense and they need to match up with what you are doing inside of your code. If you are working on your code and there is something that you want to prevent the user from doing and you want to limit the user in some way, then you will want to make an exception in there. Now that we have talked about these exceptions, it is time to take a look at an easy syntax that will help you to raise your own personal exceptions in this language:

```
class CustomException(Exception):
def_init_(self, value):
    self.parameter = value
def_str_(self):
    return report(self.parameter)

try:
    raise CustomException("This is a
CustomError!")
except CustomException as ex:
    print("Caught:", ex.parameter)
```

After you go through and add this example into your compiler, you will be able to execute it and get the result "Caught: This is a CustomError!" This will occur any time that you or someone else tries out the code. This is a good way to let the other person know that there is an exception that is going on inside of the program

With this in mind, you will be able to change up the wording so that it sounds a little bit better inside of your code. You do not need to just stick with the message that we used above. We used this right now to make things easier to work with, but you are able to add in the message that works the best for your specific code.

In addition, you are able to expand this out a little bit more and create some code that has more than one exception inside of it. This will take a few more steps to make happen, but it is not too bad. If you would like to add in two or more exceptions inside of your code, the best way to get this done is to create one class that will be the base in the code, and then that will define all of the exceptions that you would like to place in the module.

You will then be able to keep on going in order to create the right subclass that can handle all of the exceptions that you need. This will keep everything organized and will make sure that your compiler won't get confused about the exceptions that you want it to work with.

As you can see, there are a few more steps that you will need to use in order to get exceptions to work with. These are useful for ensuring that you are able to get your code to work the way that you would like. It helps you to recognize some of the exceptions that are found in the Python library, how to change the message that comes up in your code when an exception comes up, and even how to make your own exceptions. Try out a few of these examples in your compiler to see how they can work for you.

Chapter 7: Using Operators in Your Code

Another thing that you can use in your codes is known as operators. These will help you to do a few new things inside of your code, but they are usually pretty easy to work with. They can help you to compare different parts of your code, adding a value to a variable, and even to do some mathematical equations. Let's take a look at some of the different operators that you will commonly use when you are working in Python.

Arithmetic Operators

The first operator type that you will need to use on a regular basis is the arithmetic operator. They are basic, and you will use them any time that you would like the program to do some math problems. You could use these operators to help you to add two parts together or when you need to divide things up. Some of the operators that you are able to use when you want to work with the arithmetic operators include the following:

- (+): This is the addition operator
- (-): This is the subtraction operator
- (*): This is the multiplication operator
- (/): This is the division operator

You are able to use these to do any type of arithmetic equation that you want when you are in the Python code. If you decide to use more than one of these operators at the same time, you need to remember the order of operations. This means that you will need to do all the multiplication and then all the division going from left to right. Then you will do all the addition and all the subtraction to get the results that you want from these equations.

Comparison Operators

The next operator that you will want to work with inside of this coding language is called the comparison operator. This is a good one to work with when you have two or more values or statements in your code and you would like a way to bring them both together. You may see these working with Boolean expressions because they need to work on the idea of being either true or false. You will either have it that the numbers or the statements are the same, or they won't, which is how they work with Boolean expressions. Some of the comparison operators that you can use in this language include the following:

- (>=): this one means to check if the left-hand operand is greater than or equal to the value of the one on the right.

- (<=): this one means to check if the value of the left-hand operand is less than or equal to the one on the right.

- (>): this one means to check whether the values of the left side are greater than the value on the right side of the code.

- (<): this one means to check whether the values of the left side are less than the values that are on the right side.

- (!=): this is the not equal to operator.

- (==): this one is equal to operator.

As you are working on your code or your program, you may find that you use these comparison operators all the time without even realizing it. You may set up some conditions inside of your code, and you will need to make sure that these conditions are met before the code can act a specific way. When the user adds in their information, the comparison operator will be able to tell if the input given is the same or different than the conditions that you have set. You may not use this all of the time, but with conditions, as well as some other things, you will find that comparison operators are great to work with.

Logical Operators

Another option that you can go with is the logical operators. These are good ones to learn how to work with because they will take the input they are given and then evaluate it based on the conditions that you set within the code. There are several different types of operators that fit into this category, but the three logical operators that you are most likely to use include the following:

- Or: with this one, the compiler will value x, and if it is false, it will then go over and evaluate y. If x ends up being true, the compiler will return the evaluation of x.

- And: if x ends up being the one that is false, the compiler will evaluate it. If x ends up being true, it will move on and evaluate y.

- Not: if x ends up being false, the compiler will return True. But if x ends up being true, the program will return.

These logical operators are similar to the comparison operators, but you will need to use these operators in slightly different ways. You will only use the three logical operators above when you would like to make your code more powerful.

Assignment Operators

The final type of operator that you are able to work with inside of the Python language is the assignment operator. This will be the equal sign to help you to take a value and assign it over to whatever variable you are working on. For example, if you would like to take a variable and you then want to assign the value of 100 to it, you would be able to take the equal sign to complete these two together.

There are also some times when you will take the assignment operator and then use it in the code to tell you what your variable will equal. If you look through some of the codes that we have already written in this book, you can easily find a ton of these assignment operators already in use. Any time that you want to talk to the compiler and have it assign a value to your variable, you will be able to use this equal sign, or the assignment operator, to tell the compiler what value goes to it.

In addition, you have the possibility of assigning two or more values to one variable that you are working with. Doing this is pretty easy as long as you are using the right signs and you make sure that you are writing them into the code in the proper way. You can just use the same variable and assign it to each value that you want to use. In fact, your variable is able to equal as many values as you want as long as it makes sense inside of your code.

As a beginner, you may want to stick with codes that will only require one value for each of your variables. This makes it easier to write out the code, but it is not too bad if you find that you have a variable that needs to have more than one of these values go to the same variable.

It is very important that you are able to use the assignment operator. There are many times when you will have a variable and you will want to make sure that it has some meaning to it. This meaning will ensure that your variable can be called up and that it is used properly when you are working on your code. But putting a value to the variable will be almost impossible if you are not able to use the assignment operator.

Operators are an important part of the code that you are working on. The ones that we have listed above in this guidebook will make it easier for you to do some new things in your code. They may be able to add a lot of power to your code, but adding them in will be super easy. You just need to look through some of the codes that we have already done in this guidebook and even though they are basic codes for beginners, there are many operators that are found inside of them, which make it easier to work on them. Make sure to learn more about these various operators so that you can easily add them to your code.

Conclusion

Thanks for making it through to the end of this book. Let's hope it was informative and able to provide you with all of the tools you need to achieve your goals whatever they may be.

The next step is to download the Python program and the IDE that you need to work on your program. When you are done with this, you can take some time working on some of the different codes that we outlined in this guidebook. There are so many things that you are able to do with Python and the different exercises that we did in this guidebook are just the beginning of all the things that this great coding language can help you with.

Finally, if you found this book useful in any way, a review on Amazon is always appreciated!

CPSIA information can be obtained
at www.ICGtesting.com
Printed in the USA
BVHW041741030221
599227BV00013B/2527

9 791280 320155